P9-CKX-627

FUN FACT FILE:
ANIMALS!

20 FUN FACTS ABOUT
DOLPHINS

By Heather Moore Niver

Gareth Stevens
Publishing

Please visit our website, www.garethstevens.com. For a free color catalog of all our high-quality books, call toll free 1-800-542-2595 or fax 1-877-542-2596.

Library of Congress Cataloging-in-Publication Data

Niver, Heather Moore.
20 fun facts about dolphins / Heather Moore Niver.
      p. cm. — (Fun fact file. Animals!)
Includes index.
ISBN 978-1-4339-6515-9 (pbk.)
ISBN 978-1-4339-6516-6 (6-pack)
ISBN 978-1-4339-6513-5 (library binding)
1. Dolphins—Miscellanea—Juvenile literature. I. Title. II. Title: Twenty fun facts about dolphins.
QL737.C432N58 2012
599.53—dc23
                                    2011027100

First Edition

Published in 2012 by
Gareth Stevens Publishing
111 East 14th Street, Suite 349
New York, NY 10003

Copyright © 2012 Gareth Stevens Publishing

Designer: Michael J. Flynn
Editor: Greg Roza

Photo credits: Cover, pp. 1, 5, 6–7, 8 (both), 9, 10, 11, 12, 13, 14, 15, 16–17, 18, 18–19, 20, 21, 24–25, 26–27, 28, 29 Shutterstock.com; pp. 22–23 Darryl Bush/Getty Images.

Printed in the United States of America

CPSIA compliance information: Batch #CW12GS: For further information contact Gareth Stevens, New York, New York at 1-800-542-2595.

Contents

Words in the glossary appear in **bold** type the first time they are used in the text.

Dive into the World of Dolphins

Dolphins are smart, playful animals. You might see them doing flips at aquariums and zoos. Have you ever seen the black-and-white **marine** animal called a killer whale, or orca? Did you know it's really a kind of dolphin?

There are 4 river dolphin **species** and more than 30 marine dolphin species. They're all closely related to whales and porpoises. In fact, six dolphin species are often called whales, including killer whales and pilot whales. Marine dolphins are sometimes called true dolphins.

Dolphins and porpoises are part of a large group of animals called toothed whales.

Something's Fishy!

FACT 1

Dolphins live in the water, but they're not fish.

If it swims like a fish and looks like a fish, is it a fish? Not if you're talking about a dolphin! The dolphin is an **aquatic** animal, but this **mammal** needs to come to the water's surface to breathe, just like we do!

Amazon River dolphins are born gray but turn pink as they grow older.

6

KNOW YOUR DOLPHINS

Marine Dolphins

Atlantic humpbacked dolphin	Heaviside's dolphin	pantropical spotted dolphin
Atlantic spotted dolphin	Hector's dolphin	Peale's dolphin
Atlantic white-sided dolphin	hourglass dolphin	pygmy killer whale
Australian snubfin dolphin	Indo-Pacific humpback dolphin	Risso's dolphin
bottlenose dolphin	Irrawaddy dolphin	rough-toothed dolphin
Chilean (black) dolphin	long-beaked common dolphin	short-beaked common dolphin
Clymene dolphin	long-finned pilot whale	short-finned pilot whale
Commerson's dolphin	melon-headed whale	southern right-whale dolphin
dusky dolphin	northern right-whale dolphin	spinner dolphin
false killer whale	orca (killer whale)	striped dolphin
Fraser's dolphin	Pacific white-sided dolphin	white-beaked dolphin

River Dolphins

Amazon River dolphin	La Plata dolphin
Ganges and Indus River dolphin	Yangtze River (Chinese river) dolphin

What's the Difference?

People often confuse the dolphin with its cousin, the porpoise.

Dolphins and porpoises look so much alike it's hard to tell them apart. But check out their **snouts**. A dolphin's snout is longer than a porpoise's—it's more like a beak. A dolphin also has cone-shaped teeth, while a porpoise's are flatter.

dolphin snout

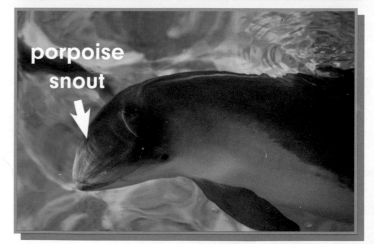

porpoise snout

Fins, Flippers, and More

Each dolphin has a fin that's different from every other dolphin's fin.

Each dolphin has a **dorsal** fin that's one of a kind—a little like your fingerprints! A dolphin's dorsal fin helps it balance in the water. It also helps the dolphin warm up or cool off. A dolphin also has two flippers that work like arms.

dorsal fin

The dolphin's tail pushes it through the water as it jumps and dives.

9

FACT 4

Dolphins' skin coloring helps them hide from enemies.

Most dolphins are black, white, and gray. When seen from above, darker skin on their back helps dolphins blend in with the water and hide from **predators**. A lighter-colored belly helps them blend in with the sky when viewed from below.

Dolphins have smooth skin that feels a bit like rubber.

blowhole

Porpoises and whales have blowholes, too.

FACT 5

A dolphin breathes through a hole on top of its head.

A dolphin's **nostril** is on top of its head! It's better known as a blowhole. The dolphin has a single blowhole. It opens when the dolphin comes up to the water's surface to breathe and closes when the dolphin dives below the surface.

A dolphin's eyes are on the sides of its head. This allows the dolphin to see what's going on all around it.

FACT 6

Dolphins can't smell their world.

Dolphins hardly have any sense of smell. They have excellent hearing, though. Scientists think that sound actually travels through their jaws. Dolphins also have very good eyesight, whether they're in or out of the water!

Speedy Swimmers, High Jumpers, and Deep Divers

Some dolphins can dive 1,000 feet (300 m) down in one breath.

Dolphins can swim about 25 miles (40 km) an hour. That's three times faster than a person can swim! Some dolphins can jump 20 feet (6 m) out of the water. Some can dive 1,000 feet (300 m) beneath the water's surface.

13

The Big and the Small

Some dolphins are about the size of a person, but others are as long as a school bus.

With so many different kinds of dolphins, of course there are lots of differences in size. The Hector's dolphin only grows to about 5 feet (1.5 m) long. The killer whale can grow up to 30 feet (9 m) long!

Dolphins at Dinner

Dolphins don't chew their food, but they're not being rude.

Dolphins don't chew their food even though they have about 100 teeth. They use these teeth to grab their food. Then they swallow it whole. Dolphins feast on most kinds of fish and sometimes even chow down on squid or shrimp.

Dolphin Chat

FACT 10

Dolphins make sounds that people can't hear.

Dolphins can locate things underwater using a process called echolocation. First, they make clicking sounds, many of which people can't hear. Then they listen for the sounds to bounce back, or echo, after hitting an object.

dolphin

HOW ECHOLOCATION WORKS

sound waves

echo

fish

Echolocation tells a dolphin how far away an object is and where it is.

FACT 11

Each dolphin has its own "name."

Dolphins can squeak, grunt, whistle, and click from the time they're born. They speak to each other with these sounds. Each dolphin has a whistle that doesn't sound like any other dolphin's. This whistle is like a name—it's how dolphins know each other.

Bumping heads is a form of dolphin body language.

Dolphins also speak by touching fins, blowing bubbles, and clapping their jaws. They even bump heads! Dolphins use this body language when they are close to each other. They let others know when food is nearby or when predators are in the area.

FACT 13

Dolphins work together to get things done.

Dolphins swim together in groups called pods. Most pods include about 12 dolphins. Sometimes pods combine to form herds containing several hundred members. Dolphins sometimes work together to get something done, such as catching fish for dinner. That's good teamwork!

These are Atlantic spotted dolphins.

FACT 14

Dolphins might be friends their whole life.

Scientists think that dolphins have long friendships with each other. Some may form a bond that lasts their whole lives! When a member of a pod is sick or dying, healthier dolphins will do what they can to help it along.

Dolphin Life

FACT 15

In 2011, the oldest known dolphin turned 58.

Female dolphins begin having babies when they're between 5 and 12 years old. They have one baby, or calf, at a time. Most dolphins live to be about 25 years old. The oldest dolphin in the world, named Nellie, turned 58 in 2011.

Dolphin calves drink their mother's milk underwater.

Baby dolphins are born tail first.

When a dolphin is born, unlike other mammals, it enters the world tail first. This way, the calf doesn't drown before the mother can push it up to the surface for its first gulp of air. A calf stays with its mother for 1 to 2 years.

Fairly Friendly Wild Animals

FACT 17

Most wild animals run from people, but dolphins seem to like human company.

Dolphins are playful and friendly. They're interested in humans, too. Sometimes they swim beside boats. But dolphins can also be forceful. Sometimes stronger dolphins pick on weaker ones. Dolphins seem friendly, but always remember they're wild animals.

Dolphins Around the World

Dolphins can be found just about anywhere on Earth there's warm water.

Dolphins like to spend their time in warm waters, usually along the coasts. Chinese river dolphins live in the Yangtze River. Peale's dolphins live along the coast of the southern tip of South America. Bottlenose dolphins live in oceans all over the world.

The bottlenose dolphin's mouth is curved so it always looks like it's smiling!

Who's Afraid of the Killer Whale?

FACT 19

The dolphin known as the killer whale doesn't kill people.

The killer whale sure has a scary name! It's the largest true dolphin and grows to about 30 feet (9 meters) long. The killer whale eats animals, but it hasn't been known to kill humans in the wild.

Dolphins in Danger

You can help keep dolphins safe.

Every year, there are fewer and fewer dolphins. They're hunted for meat. They get caught in fishing nets by mistake and drown. Polluted waters kill them. The killer whale is **endangered**.

You can help. Don't pollute. Join groups that work to keep dolphins safe. Teach others about dolphins.

Killer whales usually eat fish, but they've been known to munch on polar bears and moose!

Discovering Dolphins

Maybe you've seen dolphins at the zoo, performing at an aquarium, or in the wild. You've got to admit that they're exciting animals. Dolphins are curious creatures that may be as interested in you as you are in them.

Dolphins have been around for more than 23 million years! To keep them around, we need to keep the waters where they live safe. That way, these smart swimmers will be splashing for many more years.

Dolphins are quick learners. Trained dolphins can put on quite a show.

29

Glossary

aquatic: living, growing, or spending time in water

dorsal: on the back

endangered: in danger of dying out

mammal: a warm-blooded animal that has a backbone and hair, breathes air, and feeds milk to its young

marine: having to do with the sea

nostril: an opening through which an animal breathes

predator: an animal that hunts other animals for food

snout: a long nose that sticks out

species: a group of animals that are all of the same kind

For More Information

Books

Haney, Johannah. *Dolphins.* New York, NY: Marshall Cavendish Benchmark, 2011.

Skog, Jason. *Dolphins.* Mankato, MN: Creative Education, 2009.

Stewart, Melissa. *Dolphins.* Washington, DC: National Geographic Society, 2010.

Websites

Bottlenose Dolphins
kids.nationalgeographic.com/kids/animals/creaturefeature/bottlenose-dolphin/
Learn more about one of the most popular dolphins, the bottlenose, with facts and videos from National Geographic.

Dolphin Research Center Kids Area
www.dolphins.org/kids_area.php
This website is a great way to learn about dolphins with games, coloring, and more.

Dolphins
www.animalcorner.co.uk/marine/dolphins/dolphins_about.html
Check out facts about all different kinds of dolphins.

Index